To

From

Words to Warm a Graduate's Heart
© 2009 Summerside Press
www.summersidepress.com

Compiled by Joanie Garborg
Designed by Lisa Franke

Scripture references are from the following sources: The Holy Bible,
New International Version® NIV®. © 1973, 1978, 1984 by International
Bible Society. Used by permission of Zondervan. The NEW AMERICAN
STANDARD BIBLE® (NASB), © Copyright The Lockman Foundation
1960, 1962, 1963, 1968, 1971, 1972, 1973, 1975, 1977, 1995. Used by
permission. (www.Lockman.org). The New King James Version (NKJV).
Copyright © 1982 by Thomas Nelson, Inc. Used by permission. The
Holy Bible, New Living Translation® (NLT). Copyright © 1996, 2004.
Used by permission of Tyndale House Publishers, Inc., Wheaton,
Illinois. *The Message* © 1993, 1994, 1995, 1996, 2000, 2001, 2002.
Used by permission of NavPress, Colorado Springs, CO. The Living
Bible (TLB) copyright © 1971. Used by permission of Tyndale House
Publishers, Inc., Carol Stream, Illinois 60188. All rights reserved.

Excluding Scripture verses, references to men and masculine pronouns
have been replaced with gender-neutral references.

ISBN 978-1-934770-79-5

Printed in China

WORDS TO WARM
A
Graduate's
HEART

TABLE OF CONTENTS

· ·

Way to Go!

The tassel's worth the hassle!

You have brains in your head.
You have feet in your shoes.
You can steer yourself in
any direction you choose.
You're on your own.
And you know what you know.
You are the one
who'll decide where to go....
Just never forget
to be dexterous and deft
And never mix up
your right foot with your left.

DR. SEUSS

Keep company with God,
get in on the best.
Open up before God, keep nothing back;
He'll do whatever needs to be done:
He'll validate your life in the clear light of day.

PSALM 37:4-6 THE MESSAGE

OPTIMISM IS THE *faith* THAT LEADS TO ACHIEVEMENT. NOTHING CAN BE DONE WITHOUT HOPE AND CONFIDENCE.

HELEN KELLER

A graduation ceremony is an event
where the commencement speaker tells
thousands of students dressed in
identical caps and gowns that
"individuality" is the key to success.

ROBERT ORBEN

Achievement is the knowledge that you have studied
and worked hard and done the best that is in you.
Success is being praised by others, and
that's nice, too, but not as important or satisfying.
Always aim for achievement and forget about success.

HELEN HAYES

A span of life is nothing. But the man or woman who lives that span, they are something. They can fill that tiny span with meaning, so its quality is immeasurable, though its quantity may be insignificant.

CHAIM POTOK

At commencement you wear your square-shaped mortarboards. My hope is that from time to time you will let your minds be bold, and wear sombreros.

PAUL FREUND

To those of you who received honors, awards and distinctions, I say, "Well done." And to the "C" students, I say, "You, too, may one day be President of the United States."

GEORGE W. BUSH

His master praised him for good work. "You have been
faithful in handling this small amount," he told him,
"so now I will give you many more responsibilities.
Begin the joyous tasks I have assigned to you."

MATTHEW 25:21 TLB

THE REWARD FOR WORK WELL DONE IS THE *opportunity* TO DO MORE.

There's no thrill in easy sailing
when the skies are clear and blue,
There's no joy in merely doing things
which anyone can do.
But there is some satisfaction
that is mighty sweet to take,
when you reach a destination
that you thought you'd never make.

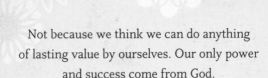

Not because we think we can do anything
of lasting value by ourselves. Our only power
and success come from God.

2 Corinthians 3:5 tlb

No matter what your age or your situation,
your dreams are achievable.
Whether you're five or 105,
you have a lifetime ahead of you!

When you leave here,
don't forget why you came.

Adlai Stevenson

New Beginnings

Each day can be the beginning of a wonderful future.

This bright, new day, complete with 24 hours
of opportunities, choices, and attitudes comes with a
perfectly matched set of 1440 minutes. This unique gift,
this one day, cannot be exchanged, replaced or refunded.
Handle with care. Make the most of it.
There is only one to a customer!

The Lord's lovingkindnesses indeed never cease,
For His compassions never fail;
They are new every morning;
Great is Your faithfulness.

LAMENTATIONS 3:22-23 NASB

Graduation is a time of completion,
of finishing, of an ending; however, it is also
a time of celebration of achievement and
a beginning for the new graduate.

CATHERINE PULSIFER

. . . .

What we feel, think, and do this moment influences
both our present and the future in ways we may
never know. Begin. Start right where you are.
Consider your possibilities and find inspiration...to add
more meaning and zest to your life.

ALEXANDRA STODDARD

THERE WILL COME A TIME WHEN YOU
BELIEVE EVERYTHING IS FINISHED.
THAT WILL BE THE *beginning*.

LOUIS L'AMOUR

Begin today! No matter how feeble the light,
let it shine as best it may. The world may need
just that quality of light which you have.

HENRY C. BLINN

WHAT WE CALL THE END IS
ALSO A *beginning*. THE END IS WHERE
WE START FROM.

T. S. ELIOT

Today is unique! It has never occurred before and
it will never be repeated. At midnight it will end,
quietly, suddenly, totally. Forever.
But the hours between now and then
are opportunities with eternal possibilities.

CHARLES R. SWINDOLL

This is the day the Lord has made;
We will rejoice and be glad in it.

PSALM 118:24 NKJV

Each of my days are miracles. I won't waste my day;
I won't throw away a miracle.

KELLEY VICKSTROM

Each morning is a fresh beginning.
Each day the world is made new. Today is
your new day when your world is made new.
You have lived all your life up to this moment
to come to this day. This moment, this day,
is as good as any moment in all eternity.
Try to make of this day—each moment
of this day—a heaven on earth.
This is your day of opportunity.

Live your life while you have it. Life is a splendid gift—
there is nothing small about it.

FLORENCE NIGHTINGALE

I like living. I have sometimes been wildly,
despairingly, acutely miserable, racked with sorrow,
but through it all I still know quite certainly
that just to be alive is a grand thing.

AGATHA CHRISTIE

We may run, walk, stumble, drive, or fly, but
let us never lose sight of the reason for the journey,
or miss a chance to see a rainbow on the way.

GLORIA GAITHER

Wisdom is sweet to your soul;
if you find it, there is a future hope for you,
and your hope will not be cut off.

PROVERBS 24:14 NIV

Life Is a School

Life is a school. There is something new to learn wherever we may be, wherever we go, wherever we turn.

WALTER A. WITT

It is important that you realize that you are not a finished product. You are still in the process of creation. In fact, all of us are in the process of creation.... But we do have a divine heritage and we are here for noble purposes. We have an infinitely important future potential, if we learn. How is it going to happen? Will it be automatic? You who are married, did the ceremony create you or qualify you as properly equipped husbands and wives? Does the birth of a baby into the family qualify you as adequate parents? Does graduation signify that we are educated?

MARION D. HANKS

YOU HAVE MADE KNOWN TO ME
THE *path* OF LIFE;
YOU WILL FILL ME WITH JOY
IN YOUR PRESENCE,
WITH ETERNAL PLEASURES
AT YOUR RIGHT HAND.

PSALM 16:11 NIV

It is indeed ironic that we spend our school days
yearning to graduate and our remaining days
waxing nostalgic about our school days.

ISABEL WAXMAN

Anyone who stops learning is old, whether at twenty or
eighty. Anyone who keeps learning stays young.

HENRY FORD

Education is a lifelong process of which schooling
is only a small but necessary part. As long as
one remains alive and healthy,
learning can go on—and should.

MORTIMER J. ADLER

The trouble with learning from experience is
that you never graduate.

DOUG LARSON

Let us think of education as the means of developing
our greatest abilities, because in each of us there is
a private hope and dream which, fulfilled, can be
translated into benefit for everyone and
greater strength for our nation.

JOHN F. KENNEDY

The person who graduates today and stops learning
tomorrow is uneducated the day after.

NEWTON D. BAKER

All of the top achievers I know are life-long learners...
looking for new skills, insights, and ideas.
If they're not learning, they're not growing...
not moving toward excellence.

DENIS WAITLEY

YOUR SCHOOLING MAY BE OVER, BUT *remember* THAT YOUR EDUCATION STILL CONTINUES.

Is life not full of opportunities for learning love?
Every man and woman every day has a thousand of them.
The world is not a playground, it is a schoolroom.
Life is not a holiday, but an education. And the
one eternal lesson for us all is how better we can love.

HENRY DRUMMOND

Show me Your ways, O Lord;
Teach me Your paths.
Lead me in Your truth and teach me.

PSALM 25:4 NKJV

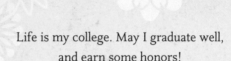

Life is my college. May I graduate well,
and earn some honors!

LOUISA MAY ALCOTT

God sets out the entire creation as a science classroom,
using birds and beasts to teach wisdom.

JOB 35:11 THE MESSAGE

I have learned that success is to be measured
not so much by the position that one has reached in life
as by the obstacles which one has overcome
while trying to succeed.

BOOKER T. WASHINGTON

God shall be my hope, my stay, my guide
and lantern to my feet.

SHAKESPEARE

Designs on Your Future

May God's love guide you through
the special plans He has for your life.

Live for today but hold your hands open to tomorrow.
Anticipate the future and its changes with joy.
There is a seed of God's love in every event,
every circumstance, every unpleasant situation in which
you may find yourself.... Allow your dreams a place in
your prayers and plans. God-given dreams can help you
move into the future He is preparing for you.

BARBARA JOHNSON

Those who build the future are those who know that
greater things are yet to come, and that they themselves
will help bring them about.

MELVIN J. EVANS

The patterns of our days are always changing...
rearranging...and each design for living is unique...
graced with its own special beauty.

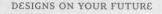
I'll take the hand of those who don't know the way,
who can't see where they're going.
I'll be a personal guide to them,
directing them through unknown country.

ISAIAH 42:16 THE MESSAGE

NEVER BE AFRAID TO *trust*
AN UNKNOWN FUTURE TO
AN ALL-KNOWING GOD.

CORRIE TEN BOOM

Joy comes from knowing God loves me and knows
who I am and where I'm going...that my future is
secure as I rest in Him.

JAMES DOBSON

We do not understand the intricate pattern of the stars
in their courses, but we know that He who created them
does, and that just as surely as He guides them, He is
charting a safe course for us.

BILLY GRAHAM

Faith MAKES THE UPLOOK GOOD,
THE OUTLOOK BRIGHT, THE
INLOOK FAVORABLE, AND
THE FUTURE GLORIOUS.

V. RAYMOND EDMAN

Those who insist upon seeing with perfect clearness
before they decide, never decide.

HENRI FRÉDÉRIC AMIEL

26

You can never change the past.
But by the grace of God, you can win the future.
So remember those things which will help you forward,
but forget those things which will only hold you back.

RICHARD C. WOODSOME

Not that I have already attained, or am already perfected;
but I press on, that I may lay hold of that for which
Christ Jesus has also laid hold of me.

PHILIPPIANS 3:12 NKJV

God has designs on our future...
and He has designed us for the future.
He has given us something to do in the future
that no one else can do.

RUTH SENTER

The uncertainties of the present always give way to the enchanted possibilities of the future.

Gelsey Kirkland

It is only a tiny rosebud—
A flower of God's design;
But I cannot unfold the petals
With these clumsy hands of mine.

For the pathway that lies before me
My Heavenly Father knows—
I'll trust Him to unfold the moments
Just as He unfolds the rose.

"For I know the plans I have for you," declares the Lord,
"plans to prosper you and not to harm you, plans to give
you hope and a future."

Jeremiah 29:11 niv

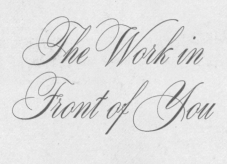

The Work in Front of You

Everything comes to him who hustles while he waits.

THOMAS EDISON

There is no hiding from work in one form
or another. Under the great sky of our endeavors
we live our lives, growing we hope, through
its seasons toward some kind of greater perspective.
Any perspective is dearly won. Maturity and energy
in our work is not granted freely to human beings
but must be adventured and discovered,
cultivated and earned. It is the result of application,
dedication, an indispensable sense of humor,
and above all a never-ending courageous conversation
with ourselves, those with whom we work,
and those whom we serve. It is a long journey,
it calls on both the ardors of youth and
the perspectives of a longer view.
It is achieved through a lifelong pilgrimage.

DAVID WHYTE

Commit to the Lord whatever you do,
and your plans will succeed.

PROVERBS 16:3 NIV

GREAT *achievements* BEGIN WITH
· SMALL OPPORTUNITIES.

The work in front of you is God's work and not yours.
If God wants it to succeed, it will. If God doesn't, it won't.
What God wants of you is to try!
So have courage—and move.

IGNATIUS OF LOYOLA

God's training is for right now, not for some
mist-shrouded future. His purpose is for this minute,
not for something better down the road. His power and
His presence are available to you as you draw your next
breath, not for some great impending struggle.
This moment is the future for
which you've been preparing!

JONI EARECKSON TADA

I studied the lives of great men and famous women,
and I found that the men and women who
got to the top were those who did the jobs they
had in hand with everything they had of
energy and enthusiasm and hard work.

HARRY S. TRUMAN

WORK *willingly* AT WHATEVER
YOU DO, AS THOUGH YOU WERE
WORKING FOR THE LORD RATHER
THAN FOR PEOPLE.

COLOSSIANS 3:23 NLT

In the business world, everyone is paid in two coins:
cash and experience. Take the experience first;
the cash will come later.

HAROLD GENEEN

Lord...give me the gift of faith
to be renewed and shared with others each day.
Teach me to live this moment only,
looking neither to the past with regret,
nor the future with apprehension.
Let love be my aim and my life a prayer.

ROSEANN ALEXANDER-ISHAM

I long to accomplish a great and noble task,
but it is my chief duty to accomplish humble
tasks as though they were great and noble.
The world is moved along, not only by
the mighty shoves of its heroes, but
also by the aggregate of the tiny pushes
of each honest worker.

HELEN KELLER

Let the favor of the Lord our God be upon us;
And confirm for us the work of our hands;
Yes, confirm the work of our hands.

PSALM 90:17 NKJV

I don't dream of wealth and success for you.
But instead, a job you like, skills you can perfect,
enthusiasm to lighten your heart, friends,
and love in abundance.

PAM BROWN

What Is Success?

The secret of success in life is...to be ready for
our opportunity when it comes.

BENJAMIN DISRAELI

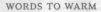

They have achieved success
who have lived well, laughed often,
and loved much;
Who [have gained] the respect
of intelligent people
and the love of little children;
Who have filled their niche
and accomplished their task;
Who have never lacked appreciation
of Earth's beauty or failed to express it;
Who have left the world
better than they found it,
Whether an improved poppy,
a perfect poem, or a rescued soul;
Who have always looked
for the best in others
and given them the best they had;
Whose life was an inspiration;
Whose memory a benediction.

BESSIE ANDERSON STANLEY

BE STRONG AND COURAGEOUS,
DO NOT BE AFRAID...FOR
THE *Lord* YOUR GOD IS THE ONE
WHO GOES WITH YOU. HE WILL NOT
FAIL YOU OR FORSAKE YOU.

DEUTERONOMY 31:6 NASB

Success is failure turned inside out,
The silver tint of the clouds of doubt,
And you never can tell how close you are,
It may be near when it seems so far.
So stick to the fight when you're hardest hit,
it's when things seem worst,
That you must not quit.

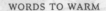

Not one word of all the good words which
the Lord your God spoke concerning you has failed;
all have been fulfilled for you, not one of them has failed.

JOSHUA 23:14 NASB

FAILURE IS ONLY THE
opportunity TO BEGIN AGAIN
MORE INTELLIGENTLY.

HENRY FORD

God...rekindles burned-out lives with fresh hope,
Restoring dignity and respect to their lives—
a place in the sun!

1 SAMUEL 2:7-8 THE MESSAGE

To dream anything that you want to dream.
That is the beauty of the human mind.
To do anything that you want to do.
That is the strength of the human will.
To trust yourself to test your limits.
That is the courage to succeed.

BERNARD EDMONDS

Enthusiasm is the element of success in everything.
It is the light that leads and the strength that
lifts people on and up in the great struggles
of scientific pursuits and of professional labor.
It robs endurance of difficulty,
and makes duty a pleasure.

W. C. DOANE

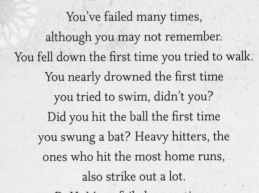

You've failed many times,
although you may not remember.
You fell down the first time you tried to walk.
You nearly drowned the first time
you tried to swim, didn't you?
Did you hit the ball the first time
you swung a bat? Heavy hitters, the
ones who hit the most home runs,
also strike out a lot.
R. H. Macy failed seven times
before his store in New York caught on.
English novelist John Creasey
received 753 rejection slips
before he published 564 books.
Babe Ruth struck out 1,330 times,
but he also hit 715 home runs.
Don't worry about failure.
Worry about the chances you miss
when you don't even try.
You don't need to have the lead
if you have the courage
to come from behind.

The Rewards of Excellence

Destiny is not a matter of chance, it is a matter of choice.
It is not a thing to be waited for; it is a thing to be achieved.

The most important moral of all is that
excellence is where you find it.
I would extend this generalization to cover
not just higher education but all education
from vocational high school to graduate school.
We must learn to honor excellence, indeed
to demand it in every socially accepted
human activity, however humble that activity,
and to scorn shoddiness, however exalted the activity.
An excellent plumber is infinitely more
admirable than an incompetent philosopher.
The society which scorns excellence in plumbing
because plumbing is a humble activity
and tolerates shoddiness in philosophy
because philosophy is an exalted activity
will have neither good plumbing
nor good philosophy.
Neither its pipes nor its theories will hold water.

JOHN W. GARDNER

Every job is a self-portrait of the person who did it. *Autograph* your work with excellence.

The price of success is hard work, dedication
to the job at hand, and the determination
that whether we win or lose, we have applied
the best of ourselves to the task at hand....
The quality of a person's life
is in direct proportion to
their commitment to excellence,
regardless of their chosen field of endeavor.

Vincent T. Lombardi

I pray that the eyes of your heart may be enlightened,
so that you will know what is the hope of His calling,
what are the riches of His inheritance in the saints,
and what is the surpassing greatness of His
power toward us who believe.

EPHESIANS 1:18-19 NASB

GO *beyond* THEIR EXPECTATIONS.
GO OUT THERE AND
DO SOMETHING ASTONISHING.

The secret of joy in work is contained in
one word—excellence. To know how to do
something well is to enjoy it.

PEARL S. BUCK

The Lord doesn't see things the way you see them.
People judge by outward appearance,
but the Lord looks at the heart.

1 Samuel 16:7 nlt

Going far beyond the call of duty,
doing more than others expect...is what
excellence is all about. And it comes
from striving, maintaining the highest standards,
looking after the smallest detail,
and going the extra mile.
Excellence means doing your very best.
In everything. In every way.

There is no road to success
but through a clear, strong purpose.

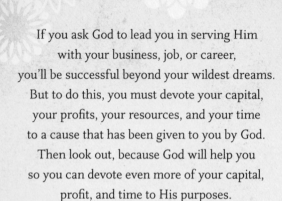

If you ask God to lead you in serving Him
with your business, job, or career,
you'll be successful beyond your wildest dreams.
But to do this, you must devote your capital,
your profits, your resources, and your time
to a cause that has been given to you by God.
Then look out, because God will help you
so you can devote even more of your capital,
profit, and time to His purposes.

LOWELL "BUD" PAXSON

The Lord has done great things for us,
and we are filled with joy.

PSALM 126:3 NIV

Lead the Way

A leader is an ordinary person with
extraordinary vision and determination.

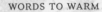

The things that haven't been done before,
Those are the things to try;
Columbus dreamed of an unknown shore
At the rim of the far-flung sky....

A few strike out, without map or chart,
Where never a man has been,
From the beaten paths they draw apart
To see what no man has seen.

There are deeds they hunger alone to do;
Though battered and bruised and sore,
They blaze the path for the many, who
Do nothing not done before.

The things that haven't been done before
Are the tasks worth while today;
Are you one of the flock that follows, or
Are you one that shall lead the way?

EDGAR A. GUEST

The measure of leadership is the caliber
of people who choose to follow you.

DENNIS A. PEER

EXAMPLE IS NOT THE MAIN THING
IN INFLUENCING OTHERS.
IT IS THE *only* THING.

ALBERT SCHWEITZER

Trust in the Lord with all your heart,
And lean not on your own understanding;
In all your ways acknowledge Him,
And He shall direct your paths.

PROVERBS 3:5-6 NKJV

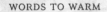
Leadership is not a one-day thing.
It is a constant commitment to excellence,
a habit...a daily practice.

A *leader* IS ONE WHO KNOWS
THE WAY, GOES THE WAY,
AND SHOWS THE WAY."

JOHN C. MAXWELL

A good leader inspires others to have
confidence in people; a great leader inspires them
to have confidence in themselves.

He who chooses the beginning of a road chooses the place
it leads to. It is the means that determine the end.

HARRY EMERSON FOSDICK

One of the best ways to persuade others is
with your ears—by listening to them.

DEAN RUSK

Surely goodness and mercy shall follow me
All the days of my life;
And I will dwell in the house of the Lord
Forever.

PSALM 23:6 NKJV

Management is doing things right; leadership
is doing the right things.

PETER F. DRUCKER

If your actions inspire others to dream more, learn more,
do more and become more, you are a leader.

JOHN QUINCY ADAMS

Don't follow the path. Go where there is no path and
begin the trail. When you start a new trail
equipped with courage, strength, and conviction,
the only thing that can stop you is you!

RUBY BRIDGES

Leadership should be born out of the understanding of the
needs of those who would be affected by it.

MARIAN ANDERSON

The best leader is the one who has sense enough
to pick good people to do what needs to be done,
and self-restraint enough to keep from
meddling with them while they do it.

Whoever wants to be a leader among you
must be your servant.

MARK 10:43 NLT

The Value of Character

What really matters is what happens in us, not to us.

D. James Kennedy

Twelve things to remember:
1) The value of time.
2) The success of perseverance.
3) The pleasure of working.
4) The dignity of simplicity.
5) The worth of character.
6) The power of kindness.
7) The influence of example.
8) The obligation of duty.
9) The wisdom of economy.
10) The virtue of patience.
11) The improvement of talent.
12) The joy of origination.

MARSHALL FIELD

Nothing is easier than saying words. Nothing is harder
than living them, day after day. What you promise today
must be renewed and redecided tomorrow and
each day that stretches out before you.

ARTHUR GORDON

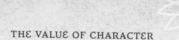

I am the Light of the world; he who follows Me will not walk in the darkness, but will have the Light of life.

JOHN 8:12 NASB

REPUTATION IS WHAT FOLKS THINK YOU ARE. PERSONALITY IS WHAT YOU SEEM TO BE. CHARACTER IS WHAT YOU *really* ARE.

ALFRED ARMAND MONTAPERT

Doing is usually connected with a vocation or a career, how we make a living. Being is much deeper. It relates to character, who we are, and how we make a life.

CHARLES R. SWINDOLL

What you do when you don't have to, determines what you will be when you can no longer help it.

RUDYARD KIPLING

55

I AM NOT BOUND TO WIN,
BUT I AM BOUND TO BE TRUE:
I AM NOT BOUND TO SUCCEED,
BUT I AM BOUND TO LIVE
UP TO WHAT *light* I HAVE.

ABRAHAM LINCOLN

The measure of a person's real character is what they would do if they knew they never would be found out.

THOMAS MACAULAY

You are right and You do right, God;
Your decisions are right on target.
You rightly instruct us in how to live
ever faithful to You.

PSALM 119:137 THE MESSAGE

We must use time creatively, and forever realize that the
time is always right to do what is right.

MARTIN LUTHER KING JR.

What people actually need is not a tensionless
state but rather the striving and struggling
for some goal worthy of them. What they need
is not the discharge of tension at any cost,
but the call of a potential meaning
waiting to be fulfilled by them.

VIKTOR FRANKL

The workshop of character is everyday life.
The uneventful and commonplace hour is
where the battle is lost or won.

MALTBIE D. BABCOCK

Character cannot be developed in ease and quiet.
Only through experience of trial and suffering
can the soul be strengthened, vision cleared,
ambition inspired, and success achieved.

HELEN KELLER

The Lord has told you what is good,
and this is what He requires of you:
to do what is right, to love mercy,
and to walk humbly with your God.

MICAH 6:8 NLT

Courage is what it takes to stand up and speak;
courage is also what it takes to sit down and listen.

SIR WINSTON CHURCHILL

A
Unique Song
to Sing

What we have done for ourselves alone dies with us;
what we have done for others and the world
remains and is immortal.

ALBERT PIKE

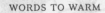

We find our greatest joy, not in getting,
but in expressing what we are.
We do not really live for honors or for pay;
our gladness is not in the taking and holding,
but in the doing, the striving, the building, the living.
It is a higher joy to teach than to be taught.
It is good to get justice, but better to do it;
fun to have things, but more to make them.
The happy person is the one who lives
the life of love, not for the honors it may bring,
but for the life itself.

R. J. BAUGHAN

Do you want to stand out? Then step down.
Be a servant. If you puff yourself up,
you'll get the wind knocked out of you.
But if you're content to simply be yourself,
your life will count for plenty.

MATTHEW 23:11-12 THE MESSAGE

You have a unique message to deliver, a unique song
to sing, a unique act of love to bestow. This message,
this song, and this act of love have been entrusted
exclusively to the one and only you.

JOHN POWELL

I PRAY THEE, O GOD, THAT
I MAY BE *beautiful* WITHIN.

SOCRATES

Whether sixty or sixteen, there is in every
human being's heart the love of wonder, the
sweet amazement at the stars and starlike things,
the undaunted challenge of events, the
unfailing childlike appetite for what-next,
and the joy of the game of living.

SAMUEL ULLMAN

Nothing important, or meaningful,
or beautiful, or interesting, or great
ever came out of imitations.
The thing that is really hard, and really
amazing, is giving up on being
perfect and beginning the
work of becoming yourself.

ANNA QUINDLEN

It's in Christ that we find out who we are
and what we are living for. Long before we
first heard of Christ and got our hopes up,
He had His eye on us, had designs
on us for glorious living, part of the
overall purpose He is working out
in everything and everyone.

EPHESIANS 1:11-12 THE MESSAGE

YOU HAVE MADE US
FOR *Yourself*, O LORD, AND
OUR HEART IS RESTLESS UNTIL
IT RESTS IN YOU.

AUGUSTINE

No one ever attains very eminent success by
simply doing what is required of him;
it is the amount and excellence of what is
over and above the required that determines
the greatness of ultimate distinction.

CHARLES KENDALL ADAMS

Jesus just wants me to allow myself to be carved into His image. The more I do, the more I realize that I become more of myself...more of who I authentically, truly, am. The more I surrender my life to Jesus, the more I actually become me.

Chynna Phillips

If you believe in God, it is not too difficult to believe that He is concerned about the universe and all the events on this earth. But the really staggering message...is that this same God cares deeply about you and your identity and the events of your life.

For in Him we live and move and have our being.

Acts 17:28 nkjv

Count Your Blessings

I want to learn to live each moment and
be grateful for what it brings, asking no more.

GLORIA GAITHER

Counting your blessings is not something
that necessarily happens in a moment,
a day, or even a year. Sometimes the blessings
that emerge from pain take an entire lifetime to
reveal themselves, and that's a good thing.
You never know when the challenge you are
facing now will become an instant "Thank God"
simply by virtue of not being as bad as
what you've already survived.

In the end, I consider myself extremely lucky.
At age nineteen, I paid tuition upfront
in the "School of Adult Life." I learned about
pain, anger, frustration, and perseverance.
Without knowing those, I wouldn't fully recognize
grace, victory, joy, beauty, peace, and gratitude.
I thank God for all of it: I am still reaping
the rewards of my Life Education.
More importantly, I'm here to tell the story.

ELIZABETH BRYAN BRENNER

The Lord bless you, and keep you;
The Lord make His face shine on you,
And be gracious to you;
The Lord lift up His countenance on you,
And give you peace.

NUMBERS 6:24-26 NASB

BE ON THE LOOKOUT FOR MERCIES.
THE MORE WE LOOK FOR THEM,
THE MORE OF THEM WE WILL SEE.
Blessings BRIGHTEN WHEN
WE COUNT THEM.

MALTBIE D. BABCOCK

Count your blessings. Learn not to take benefits,
endowments and pleasures for granted....
Thank God for them all.

J. I. PACKER

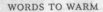

Gratitude...is not something we do at all.
Rather, it is a medium of grace, a gift of God
that softens the heart and enables it to see
and hear and receive the things
that come to it from God.

ROBERTA BONDI

FROM THE FULLNESS OF HIS *grace* WE HAVE ALL RECEIVED ONE BLESSING AFTER ANOTHER.

JOHN 1:16 NIV

Normal day, let me be aware of the
treasure you are. Let me learn from you,
love you, bless you before you depart.
Let me not pass you by in quest of some
rare and perfect tomorrow.

68

Friendships, family ties, the companionship
of little children, an autumn forest flung
in prodigality against a deep blue sky,
the intricate design and haunting fragrance
of a flower, the counterpoint of a Bach fugue
or the melodic line of a Beethoven sonata,
the fluted note of bird song, the glowing
glory of a sunset: the world is aflame
with things of eternal moment.

E. MARGARET CLARKSON

When we start to count flowers,
we cease to count weeds;
When we start to count blessings,
we cease to count needs;
When we start to count laughter,
we cease to count tears;
When we start to count memories,
we cease to count years.

Gratitude unlocks the fullness of life.
It turns what we have into enough, and more.
It turns denial into acceptance, chaos to order,
confusion to clarity.... It turns problems into gifts,
failures into successes, the unexpected into
perfect timing, and mistakes into important events.
Gratitude makes sense of our past,
brings peace for today, and creates
a vision for tomorrow.

MELODY BEATTIE

Oh, taste and see that the Lord is good;
Blessed is the man who trusts in Him!

PSALM 34:8 NKJV

May your footsteps set you upon a
lifetime journey of love.
May you wake each day with His blessings
and sleep each night in His keeping.
And may you always walk
in His tender care.

Your

Significance

God loves us for ourselves.
He values our love more than He values
galaxies of new created worlds.

A. W. TOZER

A speaker started a seminar by holding up
a twenty dollar bill. The speaker asked,
"Who would like this twenty dollar bill?"
Hands shot up all around the room. The speaker
said, "I am going to give this twenty dollar bill
to one of you, but first let me do this."
He crumpled up the twenty dollar bill and
dropped it on the ground, grinding it into the floor
with his heel. He picked it up, crumpled and dirty,
and asked, "Now who wants it?" Hands still
went up all over the room. No matter what
was done to the money, it was still desirable
because it did not decrease in value.

Many times in life, you will be dropped, crumpled,
or ground into the dirt by the circumstances that
come your way and the decisions you make.
You may feel as though you are worthless
and useless. But you will never lose your value.
Dirty or clean, crumpled or finely creased,
you are still priceless to those who love you
and to the One who made you.

Not a single sparrow can fall to the ground without your Father knowing it. And the very hairs on your head are all numbered. So don't be afraid; you are more valuable to God than a whole flock of sparrows.

MATTHEW 10:29-31 NLT

IT IS *love* WHICH
GIVES THINGS THEIR VALUE.

C. CARRETTO

Our hunger for significance is a signal
of who we are and why we are here,
and it also is the basis of humanity's enduring
response to Jesus. For He always takes
individual human beings as seriously as their
shredded dignity demands, and He has
the resources to carry through with
His high estimate of them.

DALLAS WILLARD

God made my life complete when I placed all the pieces
before Him.... God rewrote the text of my life when I
opened the book of my heart to His eyes.

PSALM 18:20, 24 THE MESSAGE

A HUMAN LIFE IS LIKE A
SINGLE LETTER OF THE ALPHABET.
IT CAN BE MEANINGLESS.
OR IT CAN BE A PART
OF A *great* MEANING.

I believe that nothing that happens to me is meaningless,
and that it is good for us all that it should be so, even if it
runs counter to our own wishes. As I see it, I'm here for
some purpose, and I only hope I may fulfill it.

DIETRICH BONHOEFFER

True worth is in *being*, not *seeming*—
In doing, each day that goes by,
Some little good—not in dreaming
Of great things to do by and by.

ALICE CARY

Half the joy of life is in little things taken on the run.
Let us run if we must—even the sands do that—
but let us keep our hearts young and our eyes open
that nothing worth our while shall escape us.
And everything is worth its while if we only
grasp it and its significance.

VICTOR CHERBULIEZ

Life varies its stories. Time changes everything,
yet what is truly valuable—what is
worth keeping—is beyond time.

RUTH SENTER

Whether sixty or sixteen, there is in every
human being's heart the love of wonder,
the sweet amazement at the stars and starlike things,
the undaunted challenge of events, the
unfailing childlike appetite for what-next,
and the joy of the game of living.

SAMUEL ULLMAN

So God created human beings in His own image;
In the image of God He created them.

GENESIS 1:27 NLT

The value of a person is not measured on an applause
meter; it is measured in the heart and mind of God....
Rest assured, for on God's scale,
the needle always reads high.

JOHN FISCHER

Something to Count On

There stands, behind all that changes and can change,
only one unchangeable joy. That is God.

HANNAH WHITALL SMITH

When we cry out with every fiber of our being,
"My soul thirsts for God, for the living God,"
then, in time, there comes a seeing that is beyond sight.
We begin to see a spiritual reality that others do not see.
And we trust in that reality, betting our lives on it.
This is what the Bible means by faith. Faith involves
an entering into the knowledge of the invisible, spiritual
world and a living on the basis of that knowledge.

RICHARD J. FOSTER

MY GOD IS *changeless*
IN HIS LOVE FOR ME
AND HE WILL COME
AND HELP ME.

PSALM 59:10 TLB

78

What gives me hope is knowing God's character,
knowing what He's like...and that He doesn't change.
Therefore, no matter what changes in my life,
no matter what the circumstances are,
I don't have to lose hope, because
I'm not trusting in my life, I'm trusting in
the One who holds my life: God.

LISA WHELCHEL

Nothing we can do will make God love us less;
nothing we do can make Him love us more.
He loves us unconditionally with
an everlasting love. All He asks of us
is that we respond to Him with the free will
that He has given to us.

NANCIE CARMICHAEL

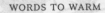
Your love, O Lord, reaches to the heavens,
Your faithfulness to the skies....
How priceless is Your unfailing love!
Both high and low among men
find refuge in the shadow of Your wings....
You give them drink from Your river of delights.
For with You is the fountain of life;
in Your light we see light.

PSALM 36:5-9 NIV

Perhaps this moment is unclear,
but let it be—even if the next, and many
moments after that are unclear, let them be.
Trust that God will help you work them out,
and that all the unclear moments will bring you
to that moment of clarity and action when
you are known by Him and know Him.
These are the better and brighter
moments of His blessing.

We are always in the presence of God....
There is never a nonsacred moment!
His presence never diminishes.
Our awareness of His presence may falter,
but the reality of His presence never changes.

MAX LUCADO

THE MORE WE *depend* ON GOD
THE MORE DEPENDABLE WE FIND HE IS.

CLIFF RICHARD

The beauty of the earth, the beauty of the sky, the order of
the stars, the sun, the moon...their very loveliness is their
confession of God: for who made these lovely mutable
things, but He who is Himself unchangeable beauty?

AUGUSTINE

What makes life worthwhile is having a
big enough objective, something which catches our
imagination and lays hold of our allegiance....
What higher, more exalted, and more compelling goal
can there be than to know God?

J. I. PACKER

Show Your marvelous lovingkindness....
Keep me as the apple of Your eye;
Hide me under the shadow of Your wings.

PSALM 17:7-8 NKJV

Guideposts on the Path

All the things in this world are gifts and signs of God's love to us.
The whole world is a love letter from God.

PETER KREEFT

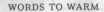

To be glad of life, because it gives you
the chance to love and to work and to play
and to look up at the stars;
to be satisfied with your possessions,
but not contented with yourself until
you have made the best of them;...
to think seldom of your enemies,
often of your friends, and every day of Christ;
and to spend as much time as you can,
with body and with spirit in God's
out-of-doors—these are little guideposts
on the footpath to peace.

HENRY VAN DYKE

WHEN WE OBEY HIM, EVERY PATH
HE GUIDES US ON IS *fragrant* WITH
HIS LOVINGKINDNESS
AND HIS TRUTH.

PSALM 25:10 TLB

I am so renewed that all nature seems renewed
around me and with me. The sky seems to be a purer,
a cooler blue, the trees a deeper green,
light is sharper on the outlines of the forest
and the hills and the whole world
is charged with the glory of God.

THOMAS MERTON

If we are children of God, we have
a tremendous treasure in nature and will
realize that it is holy and sacred.
We will see God reaching out to us
in every wind that blows, every sunrise
and sunset, every cloud in the sky,
every flower that blooms,
and every leaf that fades.

OSWALD CHAMBERS

God's bright sunshine overhead,
God's flowers beside your feet...
And by such pleasant pathways led,
May all your life be sweet.

HELEN WAITHMAN

Our Creator would never have made such lovely days,
and have given us the deep hearts to enjoy them,
above and beyond all thought, unless
we were meant to be immortal.

NATHANIEL HAWTHORNE

The Lord is my shepherd,
I shall not want.
He makes me lie down in green pastures;
He leads me beside quiet waters.
He restores my soul;
He guides me in the paths of righteousness
For His name's sake.

PSALM 23:1-3 NASB

I LOVE TO THINK OF NATURE
AS AN *unlimited* BROADCASTING
STATION THROUGH WHICH
GOD SPEAKS TO US EVERY HOUR,
IF ONLY WE WILL TUNE IN.

GEORGE WASHINGTON CARVER

I will teach you wisdom's ways
and lead you in straight paths.
When you walk, you won't be held back;
when you run, you won't stumble.
Take hold of my instructions; don't let them go.
Guard them, for they are the key to life.

PROVERBS 4:11-13 NLT

The huge dome of the sky is of all things
sensuously perceived the most like infinity.
When God made space and worlds that
move in space, and clothed our world with air,
and gave us such eyes and such imaginations
as those we have, He knew what the sky
would mean to us.... We cannot be certain that
this was not indeed one of the chief purposes
for which Nature was created....
Because God created the Natural—
invented it out of His love and artistry—
it demands our reverence.

C. S. Lewis

Always Say a Prayer

God hears your prayers,
even the ones that aren't fitting into words.

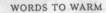
There's work to do, deadlines to meet;
You've got no time to spare,
But as you hurry and scurry
ASAP—Always Say A Prayer.

God knows how stressful life is;
He wants to ease our cares,
And He'll respond to all your needs
ASAP—Always Say A Prayer.

I CALL ON YOU, O GOD,
FOR *You* WILL ANSWER ME;
GIVE EAR TO ME
AND HEAR MY PRAYER.

PSALM 17:6 NIV

Miracles happen to those who believe in them.

FRENCH PROVERB

There are four steps to accomplishment:
Plan Purposefully.
Prepare Prayerfully.
Proceed Positively.
Pursue Persistently.

Do you believe that God is near?
He wants you to. He wants you to know
that He is in the midst of your world.
Wherever you are as you read these words,
He is present. In your car. On the plane.
In your office, your bedroom, your den.
He's near. And He is more than near.
He is active.

MAX LUCADO

Now faith is the substance of things hoped for,
the evidence of things not seen.

HEBREWS 11:1 NKJV

Always stay connected to people
and seek out things that bring you joy.
Dream with abandon. Pray confidently.

BARBARA JOHNSON

When you come to the edge of all
the light you have, and must take a step
into the darkness of the unknown,
believe that one of two things will happen.
Either there will be something solid
for you to stand on—or you
will be taught how to fly.

PATRICK OVERTON

Do not pray for an easy life. Pray to be a stronger person.
Do not pray for tasks equal to your powers. Pray for
powers equal to your tasks. Then the doing of your work
shall be no miracle, but you shall be the miracle.

PHILLIPS BROOKS

THE *prayers* WE SAY SHAPE
THE LIVES WE LIVE, JUST
AS THE LIVES WE LIVE
SHAPE THE PRAYERS WE SAY.

TED LODER

Good people are not a perfect people; good people are
honest people, faithful and unhesitatingly responsive to
the voice of God in their lives. The more often
they respond to that voice, the easier it is
to hear it the next time.

JOHN FISCHER

93

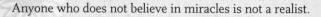

Anyone who does not believe in miracles is not a realist.

DAVID BEN-GURION

Steep yourself in God-reality, God-initiative,
God-provisions. You'll find all your everyday human
concerns will be met. Don't be afraid of missing out.
You're My dearest friends! The Father wants
to give you the very kingdom itself.

LUKE 12:31-32 THE MESSAGE

Take the first step in faith. You don't have to see
the whole staircase, just take the first step.

MARTIN LUTHER KING JR.

Faith is to believe what we do not see;
and the reward of this faith is to see what we believe.

AUGUSTINE

Make the World a Better Place

Do what you can to show you care about other people,
and you will make our world a better place.

ROSALYNN CARTER

Early one morning, an old man was standing
on the beach throwing starfish that had
washed ashore in the night back out to sea.
The man was weak and very old. Each throw
took a little more energy out of him,
but he kept on throwing. The beach was
so full of dying starfish that you could hardly
take a step without finding another.
A young man walking along the shoreline
asked the old man what he was doing.
He replied, "I'm making a difference."
The young man looked around and
laughed "A difference? There are thousands
of starfish on this beach. You can't possibly
think you will really make a difference."
The old man picked up another starfish and said,
"It makes a difference to this one..."
and threw it back into the sea.

For if you give, you will get! Your gift will return to you in full and overflowing measure, pressed down, shaken together to make room for more, and running over. Whatever measure you use to give—large or small—will be used to measure what is given back to you.

LUKE 6:38 TLB

GOD *shares* WITH THE PERSON WHO IS GENEROUS.

IRISH PROVERB

It's easy to make a buck. It's tougher to make a difference.... You are educated. Your certification is in your degree. You may think of it as the ticket to the good life. Let me ask you to think of an alternative. Think of it as your ticket to change the world.

TOM BROKAW

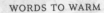
God loves me as God loves all people, without
qualification.... To be in the image of God means that all of
us are made for the purpose of knowing and loving God
and one another and of being loved in turn.

ROBERTA BONDI

One man gives freely, yet gains even more;
another withholds unduly, but comes to poverty.
A generous man will prosper;
he who refreshes others will himself be refreshed.

PROVERBS 11:24-25 NIV

NOTHING TAKEN FOR GRANTED;
EVERYTHING RECEIVED WITH
gratitude; EVERYTHING PASSED
ON WITH GRACE.

G. K. CHESTERTON

Later in my career I finally appreciated
the things that had lasting value and would
impact society for generations to come.
I noticed that most people who truly
had a positive impact on people were
others-centered and not self-centered....
People like Mother Teresa, President Lincoln,...
Martin Luther King Jr., Bill Wilson, and others,
acted out of altruistic desires to better their
generations and those to come. They made
sacrifices and gave up relatively "cushy" lives
in order to serve others and establish a legacy....

There is nothing inherently wrong in
seeking success. At the same time, I wanted to
ensure that my measure of success was
something that would lead to significance,
not necessarily in some earth-shattering
invention or contribution, but something
that would be others-centered and would serve
to benefit others in society through God's power.

RICK BREKELBAUM

Give generously, for your gifts will return to you later.
Divide your gifts among many, for in the days ahead
you yourself may need much help.

ECCLESIASTES 11:1-2 TLB

Service is the rent we each pay for living.
It is not something to do in your spare time;
it is the very purpose of life.

MARIAN WRIGHT EDELMAN

Charity is never lost: it may meet with ingratitude,
or be of no service to those on whom it was bestowed,
yet it ever does a work of beauty and grace
upon the heart of the giver.

CONYERS MIDDLETON

What Money Can't Buy

To feel rich, count all the things you have
that money can't buy.

During my second year of nursing school
our professor gave us a quiz.
I breezed through the questions
until I read the last one:
"What is the first name of the
woman who cleans the school?"
Surely this was a joke. I had seen
the cleaning woman several times,
but how would I know her name?
I handed in my paper, leaving the last
question blank. Before the class ended,
one student asked if the last question
would count toward our grade.
"Absolutely," the professor said.
"In your careers, you will meet many
people. All are significant. They deserve
your attention and care, even if
all you do is smile and say hello."
I've never forgotten that lesson.
I also learned her name was Dorothy.

JOANN C. JONES

A NEW COMMAND I GIVE YOU:
Love ONE ANOTHER.
AS I HAVE LOVED YOU, SO
YOU MUST LOVE ONE ANOTHER.

JOHN 13:34 NIV

It is said that for money you can have everything,
but you cannot. You can buy food, but not appetite;
medicine, but not health; knowledge, but not
wisdom; glitter, but not beauty; fun, but not joy;
acquaintances, but not friends; servants,
but not faithfulness; leisure, but not peace.
You can have the husk of everything for money,
but not the kernel.

ARNE GARBORG

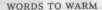

Contentment IS NOT
THE FULFILLMENT OF
WHAT YOU WANT,
BUT THE REALIZATION
OF HOW MUCH
YOU ALREADY HAVE.

At the end of your life you will never
regret not having passed one more test,
not winning one more verdict,
or not closing one more deal.
You will regret time not spent with
a spouse, a friend, a child, or a parent.

BARBARA BUSH

Let everything you say be good and helpful,
so that your words will be an encouragement
to those who hear them.

ΕΡΗΕSΙΑΝS 4:29 NLT

It's good to have money and the things that
money can buy, but it's good, too, to check up
once in a while and make sure you haven't lost
the things that money can't buy.

GEORGE HORACE LORIMER

When I get my own way, that's all I get. I don't
get the opportunity to deepen a relationship, to love
away the rough spots in a friend, or to grow spiritually.

MARIANNE JONES

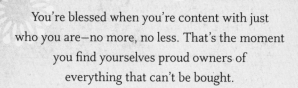

You're blessed when you're content with just
who you are—no more, no less. That's the moment
you find yourselves proud owners of
everything that can't be bought.

Matthew 5:5 the message

Gratitude is the heart of contentment.
I have never met a truly thankful, appreciative
person who was not profoundly happy.

Neil Clark Warren

First it is necessary to stand on your own two feet.
But the minute you find yourself in that position,
the next thing you should do is reach
out your arms for a friend.

Kristin Hunter Lattany

Part of a Team

No matter what accomplishments you achieve,
somebody helps you.

ALTHEA GIBSON

A man was lost while driving through the countryside.
As he tried to reach for the map, he accidentally
drove into the ditch. Though he wasn't injured,
his car was stuck deep in the mud. So the man
walked to a nearby farm to ask for help.

"Warwick can get you out of that ditch," said
the farmer, pointing to an old mule standing in a field.
The man looked at the decrepit old mule and
looked at the farmer, who just stood there repeating,
"Yep, old Warwick can do the job."

The man figured he had nothing to lose.
The two men and the mule made their way back
to the ditch. The farmer hitched the mule to the car.
With a snap of the reins, he shouted,
"Pull, Fred! Pull, Jack! Pull, Ted! Pull, Warwick!"
And the mule pulled the car right out of the ditch.

The man was amazed. He thanked the farmer,
patted the mule, and asked, "Why did you call out
all of those names before you called Warwick?"
The farmer grinned and said, "Old Warwick is nearly
blind. As long as he believes he's part of a team,
he doesn't mind pulling."

MAY GOD,
WHO GIVES THIS
PATIENCE AND
ENCOURAGEMENT,
HELP YOU LIVE IN
COMPLETE *harmony*
WITH EACH OTHER.

ROMANS 15:5 NLT

Teamwork is the ability to work together
toward a common vision. The ability to
direct individual accomplishment toward
organizational objectives. It is the fuel
that allows common people to
attain uncommon results.

ANDREW CARNEGIE

The greatest symbol of being different
in show business is pursuing excellence with
integrity and showing grace and mercy
to co-workers and other people around you.
That means not getting as frantic as others
who are desperate for their movies to work.
The Hollywood myth is that you're only
as good as your last project. But these
relationships are going to exist
no matter what...my next project is.

RALPH WINTER

COMING *together*
IS A BEGINNING; KEEPING
TOGETHER IS PROGRESS;
WORKING TOGETHER IS SUCCESS.

Blessed are the peacemakers,
for they will be called the children of God.

MATTHEW 5:9 NKJV

It is a fact that in the right formation,
the lifting power of many wings
can achieve twice the distance
of any bird flying alone.

Each of us has something different to
contribute, and no matter how small or
insignificant it may seem,
it can be for the benefit of all.

LAURITZ MELCHIOR

Our job is not to straighten
each other out, but to
help each other up.

NEVA COYLE

Since we have gifts that differ
according to the grace given to us,
each of us is to exercise them accordingly.

ROMANS 12:6 NASB

When we dream alone it remains only a dream.
When we dream together, it is not just a dream.
It is the beginning of reality.

DOM HELDER CAMARA

Hold Fast Your Dreams

Do not pray for dreams equal to your powers.
Pray for powers equal to your dreams.

ADELAIDE ANN PROCTER

Hold fast your dreams!
Within your heart
Keep one still, secret spot
Where dreams may go
And, sheltered so,
May thrive and grow
Where doubt and fear are not.
O keep a place apart,
Within your heart,
For little dreams to go!

LOUISE DRISCOLL

The important thing is to strive towards a goal
which is not immediately visible. That goal is not the
concern of the mind, but of the spirit.

ANTOINE DE SAINT-EXUPÉRY

When dreams come true at last,
there is life and joy.

PROVERBS 13:12 TLB

This is your moment! Throw off the lines.
Leave behind the safe harbor.
Catch the wind and sail into the open waters.
Seek adventure. Go after your dreams.
Discover your life.

Reach HIGH, FOR STARS LIE HIDDEN
IN YOUR SOUL. DREAM DEEP, FOR
EVERY DREAM PRECEDES THE GOAL.

PAMELA VAULL STARR

Go confidently in the direction of your dreams!
Live the life you've imagined.... You will meet with
a success unexpected in common hours.

HENRY DAVID THOREAU

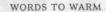

Life begins each morning....
Each morning is the open door to a new world—
new vistas, new aims, new tryings.

LEIGH MITCHELL HODGES

NO EYE HAS SEEN,
NO EAR HAS HEARD,
AND NO MIND HAS *imagined*
WHAT GOD HAS PREPARED
FOR THOSE WHO LOVE HIM.

1 CORINTHIANS 2:9 NLT

It is necessary that we dream now and then. No one
ever achieved anything, from the smallest to the greatest,
unless the dream was dreamed first.

LAURA INGALLS WILDER

The important thing really is not the
deed well done or the medal that you possess,
but the dedication and dreams
out of which they grow.

ROBERT H. BENSON

May your dreams take you to the corners of your smiles,
to the highest of your hopes, to the windows of your
opportunities, and to the most special places
your heart has ever known.

Ambition is that grit in the soul which creates
disenchantment with the ordinary and
puts the dare into dreams.

MAX LUCADO

Let stars stand for those things which are ideal
and radiant in life; if we seek sincerely and
strive hard enough, it is not impossible to reach them,
even though the goals seem distant at the onset.
And how often do we touch stars when we find them
close by in the shining lives of great souls, in the
sparkling universe of humanity around us!

ESTHER BALDWIN YORK

It's a thrill to fulfill your own childhood dreams,
but as you get older you may find that enabling the
dreams of others is even more fun.

RANDY PAUSCH

For with God all things are possible.

MARK 10:27 NKJV

A Life of Purpose

This is the true joy in life: the being used for a purpose recognized by yourself as a mighty one.

GEORGE BERNARD SHAW

If you want to know why you were placed
on this planet, you must begin with God.
You were born *by* His purpose and *for* His purpose....
How then do you discover the purpose you were
created for?... The easiest way to discover the purpose
of an invention is to ask the creator to explain it.
The same method works for discovering
your life's purpose. You can find what God,
your creator, has revealed about life in His Word,
the Bible. *Revelation* beats *speculation* any day....
There is a God who made you for a reason,
and your life has profound meaning!
We discover that meaning and purpose only when
we make God the reference point of our lives.

RICK WARREN

The Lord will fulfill His purpose for me;
Your love, O Lord, endures forever—
do not abandon the works of Your hands.

PSALM 138:8 NIV

GOD HAS A *purpose* FOR YOUR LIFE AND NO ONE ELSE CAN TAKE YOUR PLACE.

We need to set goals for ourselves.
Start today.... If you don't have any goals,
make your first goal "getting some goals."
You probably won't start living happily ever after,
but you may start living happily, purposefully,
and with gratitude.

MELODY BEATTIE

Aligning our life with God's purpose for us gives a sense
of destiny.... It gives form and direction to our life.

JEAN FLEMING

121

This is the real gift: we have been given
the breath of life, designed with a unique,
one-of-a-kind soul that exists forever—
whether we live it as a burden or a joy
or with indifference doesn't change
the fact that we've been given the gift
of *being* now and forever.
Priceless in value,
we are handcrafted by God,
who has a personal design
and plan for each of us.

THE PURPOSE OF LIFE IS A *life* OF PURPOSE.

ROBERT BYRNE

Have a purpose in life, and having it,
throw into your work such strength of
mind and muscle as God has given you.

THOMAS CARLYLE

My grace is sufficient for you,
for My strength is made perfect in weakness.

2 CORINTHIANS 12:9 NKJV

Life is so full
of meaning and purpose,
so full of beauty
—beneath its covering—
that you will find earth
but cloaks your heaven.

FRÀ GIOVANNI GIOCONDO

To develop inner strength is a pursuit
that takes time. Try to balance your outer goals
with your inner purpose, and remember
you may not be able to do everything
you think you want to do.

I will make my people strong with
power from Me! They will go
wherever they wish, and wherever they go,
they will be under My personal care.

ZECHARIAH 10:12 TLB

The highest excellence
which an individual can attain
must be to work according to the best
of his genius and to work
in harmony with God's creation.

J. H. SMYTH

Do
All the Good
You Can

The difference between ordinary and extraordinary
is that little extra.

The good you do today,
people will often forget tomorrow;
Do good anyway.
Give the world the best you have,
and it may never be enough;
Give the world the best
you've got anyway....
You see, in the final analysis,
it is between you and God;
it was never between you
and them anyway.

MOTHER TERESA

Let us not become weary in doing good,
for at the proper time we will reap
a harvest if we do not give up.
Therefore, as we have opportunity,
let us do good to all people.

GALATIANS 6:9-10 NIV

The reflective life is a way of living that prepares the
heart so that something of eternal significance can be
planted there. Who knows what seeds may come to us,
or what harvest will come of them.

KEN GIRE

NEVER LET WHAT YOU CANNOT DO *interfere* WITH WHAT YOU CAN DO.

We give thanks to God always for you,
making mention of you in our prayers;
constantly bearing in mind
your work of faith and labor of love
and steadfastness of hope.

1 THESSALONIANS 1:2-3 NASB

Do all the good you can by all the means you can
in all the ways you can in all the places
you can to all the people you can
as long as ever you can.

JOHN WESLEY

Even one day is a donation to eternity and every hour
is a contribution to the future.

Try to make each day reach as nearly as possible the high
water mark of pure, unselfish, useful living.

BOOKER T. WASHINGTON

We must not, in trying to think about how we can make
a big difference, ignore the small daily differences we can
make which, over time, add up to big differences
that we often cannot foresee.

MARIAN WRIGHT EDELMAN